AMERICAN CURL CATS

KATIE LAJINESS

Big Buddy Books
An Imprint of Abdo Publishing
abdopublishing.com

BIG BUDDY CATS

abdopublishing.com

Published by Abdo Publishing, a division of ABDO, PO Box 398166, Minneapolis, Minnesota 55439.
Copyright © 2018 by Abdo Consulting Group, Inc. International copyrights reserved in all countries.
No part of this book may be reproduced in any form without written permission from the publisher.
Big Buddy Books™ is a trademark and logo of Abdo Publishing.

Printed in the United States of America, North Mankato, Minnesota.
092017
012018

THIS BOOK CONTAINS
RECYCLED MATERIALS

Cover Photo: ZUMA Press, Inc./Alamy Stock Photo.
Interior Photos: Getty Images (pp. 5, 7, 9, 11, 13, 15, 17, 19, 21, 23, 25, 27, 29, 30).

Coordinating Series Editor: Tamara L. Britton
Contributing Editor: Jill Roesler
Graphic Design: Jenny Christensen

Publisher's Cataloging-in-Publication Data

Names: Lajiness, Katie, author.
Title: American curl cats / by Katie Lajiness.
Description: Minneapolis, Minnesota : Abdo Publishing, 2018. | Series: Big buddy cats |
    Includes online resources and index.
Identifiers: LCCN 2017943919 | ISBN 9781532111952 (lib.bdg.) | ISBN 9781614799023 (ebook)
Subjects: LCSH: American curl cat--Juvenile literature. | Cats--Juvenile literature.
Classification: DDC 636.83--dc23
LC record available at https://lccn.loc.gov/2017943919

CONTENTS

A POPULAR BREED

Cats are popular pets. About 35 percent of US households have a cat. And, Americans own more than 85 million!

Around the world, there are more than 40 **domestic cat breeds**. One of these is the American curl cat. Let's learn why the American curl is a popular cat breed.

A healthy cat can jump five to seven times its own height.

THE CAT FAMILY

All cats belong to the **Felidae** family. There are 37 **species** in this family. **Domestic cats** are part of one species. Lions and other types of cats make up the others.

Did you know?

Humans and cats have lived together for at least 3,500 years.

A male cat is called a tom. And a female cat is called a queen.

AMERICAN CURL CATS

In June 1981, Joe and Grace Ruga found a stray cat with curled ears. The couple kept the cat and named her Shulamith.

Six months later, the cat had four kittens. They were born in all colors and coat patterns. And, two of the kittens were born with their mother's curled ears!

Cat lovers called this breed the American curl because of its unusual ears.

In 1983, cat lovers began **breeding** the American curl. The breed first appeared at the **Cat Fanciers' Association** Grand Show in California. Ten years later, the breed was in the **championship** class at cat shows.

Did you know?

The American curl breed started in Lakewood, California.

Oscurl Wilde (*shown*) competed at the Iams Cat Championship at Madison Square Garden in New York City, New York.

WHAT THEY'RE LIKE

American curls are loyal and loving cats. These pets often follow their owners around the house. They get along well with children and other pets.

Did you know?
Some cats can make more than 100 different sounds!

Like dogs, the American curl can learn to play fetch.

COAT AND COLOR

These cats come in many colors, patterns, and coat lengths. This **breed** can have long, silky coats. Or, they can have short hair.

Did you know?

A cat's paw pads have more sweat glands than anywhere else on its body.

American curls often have long tufts of hair in their ears.

SIZE

At birth, an American curl's ears are straight. Within five days, the ears begin to curl back. Their position is set when the kitten is about 16 weeks old.

American curls have rectangular bodies and round eyes. The average American curl weighs five to ten pounds (2 to 5 kg).

Did you know?

The degree of ear curl ranges from almost straight to a 180-degree arc.

American curls are medium-sized cats. They are fully grown at three years old.

FEEDING

Healthy cat food includes beef, chicken, or fish. A good name-brand food will provide the **nutrients** a cat needs.

Cat food can be dry, semimoist, or canned. Food labels will show how much and how often to feed a cat.

Cats should not eat certain foods. Onions, garlic, and grapes will make them sick.

CARE

The American curl requires little **grooming**. The **breed** does not shed much. So only weekly grooming is required.

A cat should have its claws trimmed every ten to 14 days. And, it should have its ears checked to avoid germs.

Did you know?

Cats can pull back their front claws. This way, they will not scratch anyone while playing.

Happy cats massage with their paws. A kitten makes this motion when feeding from its mother.

American curls need a good veterinarian. The vet can provide health exams and **vaccines**. He or she can also **spay** or **neuter** your cat.

Kittens need to see the vet several times during their first few months. Adult cats should visit the vet once a year for a checkup.

An adult cat has 30 teeth.

Cats have an **instinct** to bury their waste. So, cats should use a **litter box**. Waste should be removed from the box daily.

A cat buries its waste to mark its area. If a cat goes outdoors, it will begin to do the same. A **microchip** can help bring a cat home if it gets lost.

Did you know?
Cats touch their noses together as a greeting.

An American curl cat's sensitive ears could be hurt by bending or tugging them.

KITTENS

An American curl mother is **pregnant** for 63 to 65 days. Then, she gives birth to a **litter** of about four kittens. For the first two weeks, kittens mostly eat and sleep.

All kittens are born blind and deaf. After two weeks, they can see and hear. At three weeks, the kittens begin taking their first steps.

Newborn kittens must be held gently.

THINGS THEY NEED

Between 12 and 16 weeks old, American curl kittens are ready for **adoption**. Kittens like to be active. So, they need daily exercise. An American curl cat will be a loving companion for about 13 years.

Jack Wright of Ontario, Canada, held the record for the most cats kept by one person. He owned 689 cats!

GLOSSARY

adoption the process of taking responsibility for a pet.

breed a group of animals sharing the same appearance and features. To breed is to produce animals by mating.

Cat Fanciers' Association established in 1906, it is the world's largest registry for pedigreed cats.

championship an event to find a first-place winner.

domestic cats tame cats that make great pets.

Felidae the scientific Latin name for the cat family. Members of this family are called felines. They include domestic cats, lions, tigers, lynx, and cheetahs.

groom to clean and care for.

instinct a way of behaving, thinking, or feeling that is not learned, but natural.

litter all of the kittens born at one time to a mother cat.

litter box a place for house cats to leave their waste.

microchip an electronic circuit placed under an animal's skin. A microchip contains identifying information that can be read by a scanner.

neuter (NOO-tuhr) to remove a male animal's reproductive glands.

nutrient (NOO-tree-uhnt) something found in food that living beings take in to live and grow.

pregnant having one or more babies growing within the body.

spay to remove a female animal's reproductive organs.

species (SPEE-sheez) living things that are very much alike.

vaccine (vak-SEEN) a shot given to prevent illness or disease.

ONLINE RESOURCES | **Booklinks** NONFICTION NETWORK
FREE! ONLINE NONFICTION RESOURCES

To learn more about American curl cats, visit **abdobooklinks.com**. These links are routinely monitored and updated to provide the most current information available.

31

INDEX